MONEY

SMALL BUSINESS OPPORTUNITIES ■ MONEY MAKING IDEAS ■ START YOUR OWN BUSINESS FOR BEGINNERS ■ ESCAPE THE RAT RACE AND BE YOUR OWN BOSS

ALEX NKENCHOR UWAJEH

LEGAL DISCLAIMERS

MONEY: SMALL BUSINESS OPPORTUNITIES - MONEY MAKING IDEAS - START YOUR OWN BUSINESS FOR BEGINNERS - ESCAPE THE RAT RACE AND BE YOUR OWN BOSS

MONEY

SMALL BUSINESS OPPORTUNITIES ■ MONEY MAKING
IDEAS ■ START YOUR OWN BUSINESS FOR BEGINNERS
■ ESCAPE THE RAT RACE AND BE YOUR OWN BOSS

CONTENTS

MONEY

SMALL BUSINESS OPPORTUNITIES ■ MONEY MAKING
IDEAS ■ START YOUR OWN BUSINESS FOR BEGINNERS
■ ESCAPE THE RAT RACE AND BE YOUR OWN BOSS

MONEY

SMALL BUSINESS OPPORTUNITIES ■ MONEY MAKING IDEAS ■ START YOUR OWN BUSINESS FOR BEGINNERS ■ ESCAPE THE RAT RACE AND BE YOUR OWN BOSS

INTRODUCTION

Deciding to start a business can be one of the most exciting decisions you'll make in your lifetime. Being your own boss can be an extremely fulfilling experience, both professionally and personally.

However, there's also plenty of work involved in creating a successful business enterprise.

MONEY

**SMALL BUSINESS OPPORTUNITIES ■ MONEY MAKING
IDEAS ■ START YOUR OWN BUSINESS FOR BEGINNERS
■ ESCAPE THE RAT RACE AND BE YOUR OWN BOSS**

Fortunately, there are some types of businesses that can be established relatively easily and without a big investment to get you started. If you set up your business plan right in the beginning, it's also possible to build your business into a million dollar empire.

The key is to find a business and an industry that you are passionate about, and then test the waters on a part-time basis. Some of the world's most successful businesses began as part-time ideas in someone's living room or basement or garage that grew into major corporations over time.

Throughout this book, we'll also look at some million-dollar-business case studies that began

MONEY
SMALL BUSINESS OPPORTUNITIES ■ MONEY MAKING
IDEAS ■ START YOUR OWN BUSINESS FOR BEGINNERS
■ ESCAPE THE RAT RACE AND BE YOUR OWN BOSS

as small operations and grew into large corporations.

Are you ready to look into some business ideas?

MONEY

**SMALL BUSINESS OPPORTUNITIES ■ MONEY MAKING
IDEAS ■ START YOUR OWN BUSINESS FOR BEGINNERS
■ ESCAPE THE RAT RACE AND BE YOUR OWN BOSS**

PARTY SERVICES

Everybody wants their parties to be memorable, but they often don't have the time or the ability to organize everything that needs to be done to create such an event. Of course, they also want a way to memorialize the event

MONEY

SMALL BUSINESS OPPORTUNITIES ■ MONEY MAKING IDEAS ■ START YOUR OWN BUSINESS FOR BEGINNERS ■ ESCAPE THE RAT RACE AND BE YOUR OWN BOSS

too so they can look back on it some day and remember fun times.

Offering party services allows others to spend more time socializing and enjoying the event without the stress of planning, organizing, cooking, serving, taking photos or videos, or otherwise trying to find activities or entertainment to help keep the party going.

Party Planning Services

As a party planner, your job is to create some of the most memorable moments in people's lives. A party planner organizes a particular party, gathering, or event in line with the customer's preferences.

As your own boss, you have the option of offering to plan all types of parties, or you can choose to specialize in specific types of parties that you enjoy the most. Some options open to you include:

MONEY

SMALL BUSINESS OPPORTUNITIES ■ MONEY MAKING
IDEAS ■ START YOUR OWN BUSINESS FOR BEGINNERS
■ ESCAPE THE RAT RACE AND BE YOUR OWN BOSS

- Anniversary party
- Baby showers
- Birthday parties
- Children's parties
- Cocktail or dinner parties
- Corporate parties and functions
- Engagement parties
- Family reunions
- Retirement parties
- Themed parties and events
- Wedding showers and wedding receptions

MONEY
SMALL BUSINESS OPPORTUNITIES ■ MONEY MAKING
IDEAS ■ START YOUR OWN BUSINESS FOR BEGINNERS
■ ESCAPE THE RAT RACE AND BE YOUR OWN BOSS

You can choose to offer full service party planning, where you arrange and handle every detail of the party, right from décor and decorations, to activities and entertainment, through to catering and service for food and drink. Most planners who offer full service also attend the party to ensure everything runs smoothly.

Alternatively, you might want to specialize in just certain aspects of the party, such as arranging catering, or refreshments and beverages, or just the décor and decorations, or just venue location.

Before you get started, you'll need to look into what licenses some state and local governments require. You may also want to invest in liability insurance to protect you in the event that a guest is injured or causes damage to the party venue.

You'll also need to spend some time putting together a list of potential new business contacts to help you supply your parties. For

example, you'll need access to a list of reliable local caterers, photographers, suppliers, and entertainers, along with access to a range of different venue options.

CLEANING SERVICES

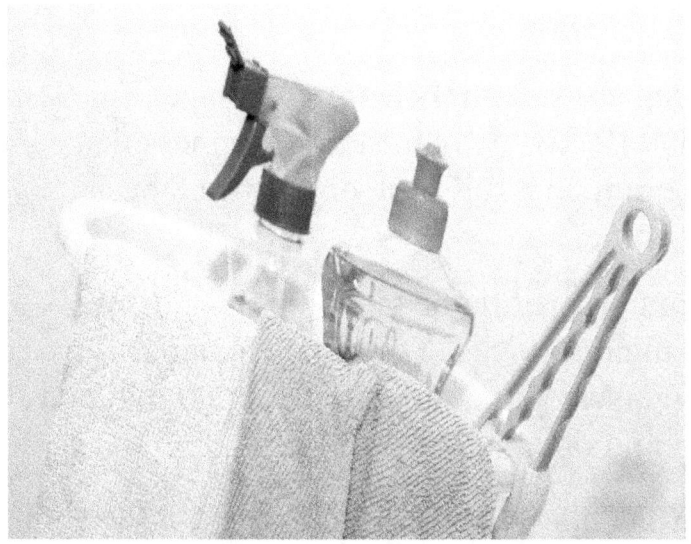

Cleaning services are always in demand. If it can get dirty, there is someone out there willing to pay you to clean it. In fact, professional cleaning is one of the few industries with such a wide variety of opportunities to start your own business for a small cost outlay.

MONEY

**SMALL BUSINESS OPPORTUNITIES ▪ MONEY MAKING
IDEAS ▪ START YOUR OWN BUSINESS FOR BEGINNERS
▪ ESCAPE THE RAT RACE AND BE YOUR OWN BOSS**

Home Cleaning

Starting a residential cleaning service is a highly effective way to start a business that can be run on a full-time or part-time basis from home.

The majority of home cleaning businesses offer maid services. You'll be cleaning, dusting, sweeping, mopping, vacuuming, and scrubbing other people's homes.

Many people start out offering their services to friends, neighbors, or family members. If you do a good job in their homes, some of them are likely to recommend your services to other people, which is a great way to increase your customer base.

Alternatively, you can put flyers into neighborhood mailboxes advertising your services in your local area.

You'll need to transport your own cleaning materials to each job, including a broom, a mop, cleaning products, sponges, and a squeegee. Some customers may let you use their regular household vacuum cleaner. Others may request that you bring one instead.

Commercial Cleaning

If you're willing to work at times when others don't, you could start a commercial cleaning service. Many business owners will happily pay someone to come in and clean their offices or stores  after normal working hours.

Some commercial businesses may need you to provide basic janitorial services, such as mopping and polishing floors, vacuuming,

MONEY

SMALL BUSINESS OPPORTUNITIES ■ MONEY MAKING IDEAS ■ START YOUR OWN BUSINESS FOR BEGINNERS ■ ESCAPE THE RAT RACE AND BE YOUR OWN BOSS

emptying garbage bins, and cleaning staff kitchen and toilet facilities.

You will need some tools to complete your job, including a commercial-grade vacuum cleaner, a floor buffer, rubber gloves, a mop, bucket, sponges, a squeegee, garbage bags, and cleaning products.

You can hand out your business card or your flyer advertising your services to local businesses, or send out your flyer in a direct mail campaign to gain new customers.

Carpet Cleaning

It's common for people to put off until later any chore that needs special equipment. Carpet cleaning is one of those tasks. Homeowners know the importance of maintaining their carpets, but many are afraid to use the rented do-it-yourself carpet shampoo machines or steam cleaning machines for fear of damaging them.

MONEY

SMALL BUSINESS OPPORTUNITIES ■ MONEY MAKING
IDEAS ■ START YOUR OWN BUSINESS FOR BEGINNERS
■ ESCAPE THE RAT RACE AND BE YOUR OWN BOSS

You will need to buy some equipment before you get started. You'll need a carpet extraction machine, a carpet cleaning wand with at least two jets, jet upholstery tool, a stair cleaning tool, a slow speed scrubber, carpet grooming rake, corner guards, carpet pre-spray solution, and acid rinse conditioner. You'll also need to take out general liability insurance for your business.

Window Cleaning

Window cleaning is an excellent business for anyone on a shoestring budget. You can get started with only a small cash outlay and be in business almost immediately.

MONEY

SMALL BUSINESS OPPORTUNITIES ■ MONEY MAKING IDEAS ■ START YOUR OWN BUSINESS FOR BEGINNERS ■ ESCAPE THE RAT RACE AND BE YOUR OWN BOSS

You will need a bucket, sponge, window scrubber, squeegee, and window cleaning soap. If your customers have two-story homes or offices you might also need an extension pole for your scrubber and squeegee, or a ladder.

Residential customers may not always be regular about booking your services, but they can form a healthy part of your overall income.

By comparison, commercial customers are far more likely to book your services on a regular basis. Owners of offices, restaurants, or retail stores like to keep their businesses looking

MONEY

SMALL BUSINESS OPPORTUNITIES ■ MONEY MAKING
IDEAS ■ START YOUR OWN BUSINESS FOR BEGINNERS
■ ESCAPE THE RAT RACE AND BE YOUR OWN BOSS

clean and fresh, so approach local businesses and let them know about your services.

Gardening and Lawn Care

Lawn and garden care services are always popular. After all, homeowners want their homes to look good, but they don't always have the time to get out and look after the lawns or garden beds.

Your job will be to mow, edge, trim, and fertilize lawns for around 20 to 30 clients each week. Some clients may also ask you to maintain garden beds by pulling weeds, pruning bushes and trees, or just keeping the garden looking neat and tidy.

MONEY

SMALL BUSINESS OPPORTUNITIES ■ MONEY MAKING IDEAS ■ START YOUR OWN BUSINESS FOR BEGINNERS ■ ESCAPE THE RAT RACE AND BE YOUR OWN BOSS

You'll need a well-maintained lawn mower, a lawn edger, leaf blower, and a rake. You may also need a truck or trailer to transport your tools and equipment to each customer's home, along with offering the option of removing grass clippings for those customers who want this service.

Lawn care is a seasonal business, with some downtime during late fall and winter for around two-thirds of the country. Prime lawn growing months are usually from April to early October.

As the grass-growing season is limited to certain times throughout the year, you have the option of working longer hours during spring and summer to build up your income and your customer base.

If you're careful about marketing your services aggressively enough throughout the lawn care season, you should be able to put aside enough funds to carry you through the income-free winter months.

MONEY

SMALL BUSINESS OPPORTUNITIES ■ MONEY MAKING IDEAS ■ START YOUR OWN BUSINESS FOR BEGINNERS ■ ESCAPE THE RAT RACE AND BE YOUR OWN BOSS

Alternatively, you could expand your services to include other seasonal activities. You could offer existing clients gutter cleaning services through fall and snowplowing or snow shoveling services through winter if you're keen to continue working.

You should find that clients who are already happy with your lawn care services throughout the rest of the year will see the benefit in continuing to hire you for other services through down times too.

Gutter Cleaning

Most people dread cleaning their home gutters, but it is an essential chore that must be done regularly. If you're willing to do the job, there's plenty of business out there and demand is always high.

Cleaning gutters involves removing any debris that has built up in the rain gutters of residential homes. The gunk that builds up in gutters can stain anything it touches, so you'll

MONEY

SMALL BUSINESS OPPORTUNITIES ■ MONEY MAKING IDEAS ■ START YOUR OWN BUSINESS FOR BEGINNERS ■ ESCAPE THE RAT RACE AND BE YOUR OWN BOSS

need to remove it from the gutter using a scoop or your hands and place it into a bucket to be disposed of once you're on the ground again.

Your biggest expenses when starting a gutter cleaning business will be ladders. You'll also need to invest in good safety ropes, a harness, and a lanyard to protect yourself against falling. It's also a good idea to consider protecting yourself with insurance, as you'll be working on ladders and rooftops.

The rest of your equipment and tools are easy. You'll need heavy rubber gloves, gutter scoop, heavy garbage bags, and a 5-gallon bucket.

Distribute flyers to homes in your local area at least a month before gutter cleaning season begins. Neighborhoods with lots of large, leafy trees near homes are ideal.

Keep in mind that gutter cleaning is a seasonal business, so you'll only be working through some periods of the year. In many parts of the country, autumn is gutter-cleaning time.

MONEY

SMALL BUSINESS OPPORTUNITIES ■ MONEY MAKING
IDEAS ■ START YOUR OWN BUSINESS FOR BEGINNERS
■ ESCAPE THE RAT RACE AND BE YOUR OWN BOSS

However, as the demand for gutter cleaning is so high, you have the potential to earn a substantial amount of money over a short period of time. If you have a lawn care business that slows down in the fall, gutter cleaning is a great way to supplement your income.

Snow Removal Services

 Snow removal services are definitely a seasonal business, but there is the potential to earn a substantial income in a short period of time. Your job is to remove built up snow from sidewalks, driveways, and pathways to a customer's home so they don't have to. It's common to hear of snowplow operators earning $1,000 per day when the snow is blowing.

MONEY

**SMALL BUSINESS OPPORTUNITIES ■ MONEY MAKING
IDEAS ■ START YOUR OWN BUSINESS FOR BEGINNERS
■ ESCAPE THE RAT RACE AND BE YOUR OWN BOSS**

You can attach a snow blade to your mower or your truck and offer snowplowing services. For snow and ice removal services, you'll also need a shovel, a salt spreader for de-icing, and a self-propelled snow blower.

Start advertising your snow removal services to existing customers and other people within the local at least a month before winter sets in. If you already have a lawn care service, this is a great option to supplement your income through the winter months.

Of course, if you pick up new customers through winter, chances are they'll continue to book you for your other services through the spring, summer, and fall months too.

MONEY

SMALL BUSINESS OPPORTUNITIES ■ MONEY MAKING IDEAS ■ START YOUR OWN BUSINESS FOR BEGINNERS ■ ESCAPE THE RAT RACE AND BE YOUR OWN BOSS

Car Cleaning and Auto Detailing Services

Car cleaning and auto detailing services are in high demand. Anyone with a car who wants to keep it looking good and has the income to pay for your services is a potential customer.

Your job is to wash, and wax other people's cars. You'll be vacuuming and shampooing carpets, cleaning upholstery, polishing chrome and cleaning tires.

The big advantages of having a car cleaning business are that you can start it on a shoestring budget and you can choose to run it part-time, if that suits your schedule.

MONEY

SMALL BUSINESS OPPORTUNITIES ■ MONEY MAKING IDEAS ■ START YOUR OWN BUSINESS FOR BEGINNERS ■ ESCAPE THE RAT RACE AND BE YOUR OWN BOSS

Your equipment will include a wet/dry vacuum, a mini-carpet shampooer, a buffer or polisher, brushes, sponges, buckets, soap, window cleaner, and wax. You'll also need a vehicle to cart all your tools around in.

You will need to know which car cleaning products are safe for what types of finishes and which ones produce the best results. It's also fairly intensive labor, so you'll need to be fit and healthy enough to keep at it.

Ironing / Mobile Laundry Service

Let's face it: busy people will pay you to do the tasks they're too busy to complete. If you're willing to offer ironing or mobile laundry services to busy people, they'll pay your fee for the convenience of getting it done.

Most people dread the idea of ironing, but it's an essential part of life, so they'll figure that it's better to pay someone else to do it than to do it themselves.

You'll need the tools of your trade in order before you begin your business. At the very least, you'll need an iron and an ironing board. Once you expand your business operations, an ironing steam generator would be a good investment, as you can complete more items in a faster time frame.

A water descaler is also a good idea if you're using your iron for more than just regular home usage. It's worth the investment to stop your iron or steam generator from breaking down when you need it most.

Marketing your services should be relatively easy. You can start with flyers delivered to local homes within your neighborhood. You can also let word of mouth spread knowledge of your home business enterprise to gain new customers.

MONEY

SMALL BUSINESS OPPORTUNITIES ■ MONEY MAKING
IDEAS ■ START YOUR OWN BUSINESS FOR BEGINNERS
■ ESCAPE THE RAT RACE AND BE YOUR OWN BOSS

Work out your pricing and set a schedule of fees for the type of clothing items you're willing to iron. It's also a good idea to create some simple business policies about the types of clothing you won't accept for your business.

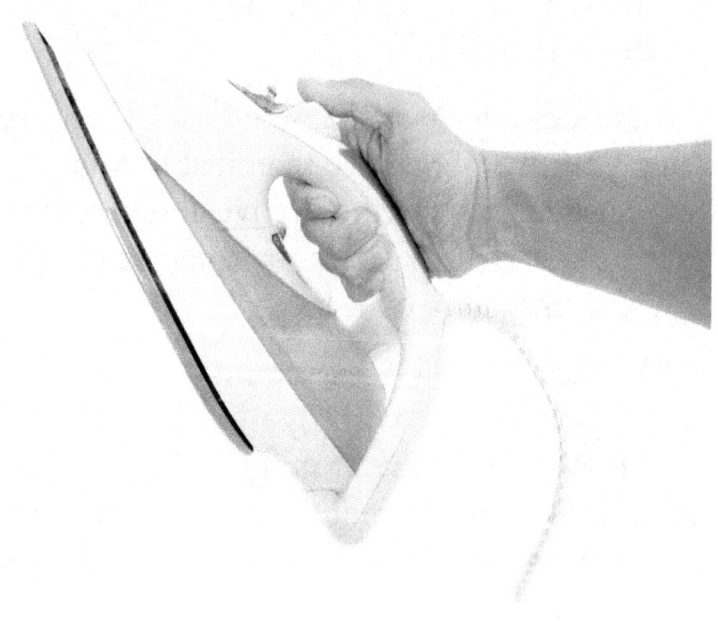

MONEY

SMALL BUSINESS OPPORTUNITIES ■ MONEY MAKING IDEAS ■ START YOUR OWN BUSINESS FOR BEGINNERS ■ ESCAPE THE RAT RACE AND BE YOUR OWN BOSS

If possible, try to avoid charging by the hour for ironing services, as most people simply assume you'll take your time completing their chores. Set a price per item for your services so people can estimate their costs before they engage your services.

MONEY

SMALL BUSINESS OPPORTUNITIES ■ MONEY MAKING IDEAS ■ START YOUR OWN BUSINESS FOR BEGINNERS ■ ESCAPE THE RAT RACE AND BE YOUR OWN BOSS

FOOD BUSINESSES

If you've had countless compliments on your cupcakes, or you have people begging you to tell them your secret recipes for their favorite dishes, you might be able to turn your skills into a profitable business.

Starting a restaurant to showcase your culinary skills is expensive, but there are some more affordable options that offer an excellent way to launch a new food business idea.

MONEY
**SMALL BUSINESS OPPORTUNITIES ■ MONEY MAKING
IDEAS ■ START YOUR OWN BUSINESS FOR BEGINNERS
■ ESCAPE THE RAT RACE AND BE YOUR OWN BOSS**

No matter what food business you decide to start, you do need to obtain the necessary licenses and permits you'll need in order to sell food. Each state has their own individual permits and licensing requirements, so take some time to check what needs to be done.

You may also need to obtain permits to park your cart or truck on streets, near arenas or stadiums, at college campuses, in the business district, in a park or a mall, or on a beach property.

Food Kiosks and Carts

Food carts have been around for decades, but modern day carts have really cleaned up the image of street-food vendors. It's common to see foods such as hot-dogs, kebobs, or ice creams sold from carts, although there are plenty of other types of food carts around as well.

Food kiosks are often temporary stands or mobile booths designed for selling food. It's

common to find pop-up food kiosks in flea markets, malls, movie theaters or stadiums.

Food carts are easy to maintain and much cheaper to get started, as compared to a food truck. There is also less licensing to worry about with a food cart than there is with other types of food trucks.

The highly mobile nature of a food cart means you can shift location to suit your customer base, or move around to suit weather conditions. Owning a food cart gives you the freedom to expand your customer base in new locations too. You can cash in on big events by temporarily placing your food cart near a stadium or conference center.

You will still need to obtain the necessary permits before you start trading. In some locations, you may also have to pay for rent on the street, in the mall, or at an event.

MONEY

SMALL BUSINESS OPPORTUNITIES ■ MONEY MAKING
IDEAS ■ START YOUR OWN BUSINESS FOR BEGINNERS
■ ESCAPE THE RAT RACE AND BE YOUR OWN BOSS

Food Truck Business

According to research conducted in Los Angeles, the street-food business is a $1 billion industry. The study included mobile food trucks, food carts, trailers, and kiosks that have popped up all over the country.

Food trucks have much lower start-up costs and operating overheads than running a brick-and-mortar restaurant, but a well-equipped food truck is considerably more expensive than a cart or kiosk.

Most food trucks do great business in corporate parks and other places with limited access to restaurants. If one location isn't generating enough income, you have the ability to move to a new location with better prospects.

Food trucks that offer specialty food and gourmet dishes also do very well in some

MONEY

SMALL BUSINESS OPPORTUNITIES ■ MONEY MAKING
IDEAS ■ START YOUR OWN BUSINESS FOR BEGINNERS
■ ESCAPE THE RAT RACE AND BE YOUR OWN BOSS

areas. Specialty trucks usually focus on serving food not typically found in traditional food trucks.

Gourmet Snack Food

Packaging and selling your own homemade soup, jam, candy, salsa, or popcorn is easier than ever in recent times. Customers are always willing to try your new taste sensation and there are plenty of outlets available to start building up your customer base.

Of course, there is a range of health regulations, state laws, and rules you'll need to abide by if you hope to be successful. You may also be visited at random by health inspectors to ensure the food you're preparing, handling, and packaging is safe for

MONEY
SMALL BUSINESS OPPORTUNITIES ■ MONEY MAKING
IDEAS ■ START YOUR OWN BUSINESS FOR BEGINNERS
■ ESCAPE THE RAT RACE AND BE YOUR OWN BOSS

your customers to consume. They also check that your manufacturing facilities are clean and meet stringent regulations.

Surprisingly, starting your own gourmet snack food business is relatively cost effective. You can begin operations right from your own kitchen bench. Until recently, many states banned the sale of any food made in a home kitchen.

You will need to be very careful about the ingredients you're able to use in your food products. You'll also need to be vigilant about your labeling, the types of foods you can sell, and where products can be sold.

For example, the US Department of Agriculture (USDA) has strict rules about food labels. You must list all the ingredients used in the manufacture of the product and the nutritional content, including calories, fat, cholesterol, proteins, and vitamins.

MONEY

SMALL BUSINESS OPPORTUNITIES ■ MONEY MAKING
IDEAS ■ START YOUR OWN BUSINESS FOR BEGINNERS
■ ESCAPE THE RAT RACE AND BE YOUR OWN BOSS

As your snack food enterprise grows, you also have the option of renting commercial kitchen premises.

While some entrepreneurs may happily approach retail outlets and chains to stock their products while they're still small, others may find that testing the market response works better for them.

Setting up a small food stall or kiosk at a flea market or farmer's market is a great way to test market response to your products before you spend too much money on creating huge batches of product. You'll also be earning some money back into the business while you develop your product lines.

There's also the advantage of getting your product out in front of people who have the potential of turning into loyal customers over the long term.

Once you're sure that the market is favorable to your products, go ahead and approach stores, chains, and other distributors to sell

MONEY

SMALL BUSINESS OPPORTUNITIES ■ MONEY MAKING IDEAS ■ START YOUR OWN BUSINESS FOR BEGINNERS ■ ESCAPE THE RAT RACE AND BE YOUR OWN BOSS

your homemade gourmet snack food products on their shelves for you.

Mobile Catering Service

Offering a mobile catering service allows you to take your business directly to your customers. Most catering services transport the food to the event that are usually served on trays or buffet style.

The advantage of a mobile catering service over a food truck is that you don't risk as much in inventory as you're only cooking and bringing food to cater for the number of people at the party or event.

You also have the advantage of not having to worry if a particular destination will be busy or not, as you already know how many people will be at your destination.

MONEY

SMALL BUSINESS OPPORTUNITIES ■ MONEY MAKING
IDEAS ■ START YOUR OWN BUSINESS FOR BEGINNERS
■ ESCAPE THE RAT RACE AND BE YOUR OWN BOSS

Million Dollar Case Study #1

Janine Allis had a dream of providing healthy juice and smoothies to customers. She began her business enterprise on her kitchen bench.

When she was ready to take the leap, her fruit juices and smoothies were first sold in a small food kiosk located in Adelaide, South Australia in 2000. The entrepreneur worked hard to ensure her little store thrived, building it into a profitable enterprise.

Since that time, her little juice business has expanded to include more than 350 Boost Juice franchises in more than 15 countries around the world, from Australia, to Portugal, Russia, Singapore, India, Chile, Germany, Dubai, and the United Kingdom.

Franchising agreements for the juice bar have also been secured in Mexico, China and Thailand.

MONEY

SMALL BUSINESS OPPORTUNITIES ■ MONEY MAKING
IDEAS ■ START YOUR OWN BUSINESS FOR BEGINNERS
■ ESCAPE THE RAT RACE AND BE YOUR OWN BOSS

Million Dollar Case Study #2

Angie Bastian was a mother of two who hoped to earn a little bit of extra cash part-time to put into her kids' college funds, but her little idea expanded into a $50 million business.

Angie grew up eating popcorn done created by her mother as a weekend tradition. She wanted to bring some of their favorite flavor combinations to other people, so she bought some kettle corn equipment and experimented with different flavors until she landed on some winners.

When she had her special recipe just right, she convinced a storeowner to allow her to set up a small food stall outside a grocery store. Within the first three hours her little stall made $300.

She expanded operations to set up her stall outside amateur baseball games in the

MONEY

SMALL BUSINESS OPPORTUNITIES ■ MONEY MAKING
IDEAS ■ START YOUR OWN BUSINESS FOR BEGINNERS
■ ESCAPE THE RAT RACE AND BE YOUR OWN BOSS

evenings and out from of the local Home Depot store on weekends.

Before long, the Minnesota Vikings were asking if Angie's Popcorn could become the official popcorn snack for the team. Everyone wanted to know where they could buy it.

At that point, Angie and her family went from being food stall vendors to manufacturers of the massively popular Angie's Popcorn brand. They added 50 kettles to their modest little operation and expanded to hire 150 employees. By that point, the Angie's Popcorn brand was being sold on the shelves at Costco and Target.

MONEY

SMALL BUSINESS OPPORTUNITIES ■ MONEY MAKING
IDEAS ■ START YOUR OWN BUSINESS FOR BEGINNERS
■ ESCAPE THE RAT RACE AND BE YOUR OWN BOSS

PET BUSINESSES

Many pet owners treat their pets just like their children. They want the best care options, the best food options, and the best lifestyle they can provide for their beloved pets.

Providing products or services for pets is a growing industry. After all, Americans spend more than $30 billion annually on their pets.

If you love animals and you want to create a business that revolves around pets, you have a huge number of options available to you.

Pet Sitting

There are many pet owners who can't leave a pet at a boarding kennel or with friends or family. The pet may have a chronic health

MONEY

SMALL BUSINESS OPPORTUNITIES ■ MONEY MAKING IDEAS ■ START YOUR OWN BUSINESS FOR BEGINNERS ■ ESCAPE THE RAT RACE AND BE YOUR OWN BOSS

condition, or it may be an exotic pet that is difficult to take care of.

Then there are people who prefer to keep their pet in a familiar, safe environment, rather than sending them to an unfamiliar boarding facility, so they'll hire a pet sitter to be at home when they're not.

Some people also hire pet sitters for short periods of time, such as a night out, or a day off. No matter what your customers' reasons are, there is definitely a market for good pet sitting services.

You can market your pet sitting services through other pet-related businesses in your area. For example, vets, dog grooming salons, dog training centers or local pet stores.

MONEY

**SMALL BUSINESS OPPORTUNITIES ■ MONEY MAKING
IDEAS ■ START YOUR OWN BUSINESS FOR BEGINNERS
■ ESCAPE THE RAT RACE AND BE YOUR OWN BOSS**

Dog Day Care

Dog day care facilities are incredibly popular with owners who don't want to leave their dogs at home alone while they're at work. Dogs are highly social creatures and need contact and interaction throughout the day.

A dog day care center is designed for owners to drop off their pet in the morning and pick them up again in the evening. It's not intended to be a long-term boarding kennel, so there are no overnight stays.

If you have sufficient space and a securely enclosed yard, you can start your business at home.

However, a better alternative is to rent a warehouse that has a securely fenced outdoor space and convert it into a day care facility. You can provide comfortable indoor areas for

MONEY

SMALL BUSINESS OPPORTUNITIES ■ MONEY MAKING IDEAS ■ START YOUR OWN BUSINESS FOR BEGINNERS ■ ESCAPE THE RAT RACE AND BE YOUR OWN BOSS

dogs, including lounges and beds, play areas inside and outside with dog-safe toys, or even add water features.

Install some web-cams around the indoor and outdoor areas and connect them to a private area of your website. Owners who want to check what their dogs are doing through the day can log in and view footage of their dogs playing or sleeping or just doing what dogs do.

Pet Photography

If you're good with photography, what better way to earn a living than by photographing people's beloved pets? You can operate on a mobile basis, or from a home-based studio, or from pet shops, or a combination of all three.

Owners want to create precious memories of their pets, so make your photography service fun and interesting by offering themed backdrops, costumes, or other ways to ensure your customers look amazing in each photo you take.

You also have the option of boosting your profits by offering other products that allow customer to transfer their pet photos onto. For example, you can offer calendars, greeting cards, t-shirts, or mugs to customers that have their pets' photos transferred onto.

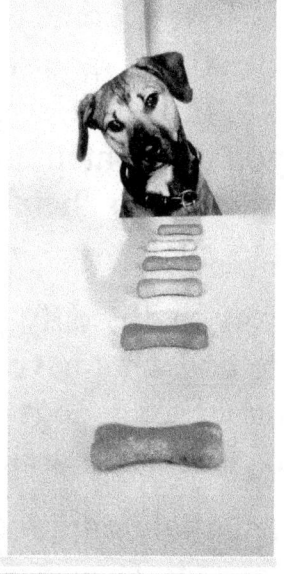

Gourmet Pet Treats

The fastest growing area in the pet food industry is gourmet dog treats. People love their

MONEY

SMALL BUSINESS OPPORTUNITIES ■ MONEY MAKING
IDEAS ■ START YOUR OWN BUSINESS FOR BEGINNERS
■ ESCAPE THE RAT RACE AND BE YOUR OWN BOSS

dogs and they want the very best dog treats they can find.

Most pet owners are aware that commercially bought treats and pet foods often contain preservatives, artificial colorings and flavorings, and other fillers. In an effort to ensure their pets are eating a healthy diet, owners seek out pet treats containing natural ingredients.

Creating your dog treats at home is relatively easy. You'll need some recipes, some molds to create cute shapes, and some packaging materials. You will need to check that any recipes you use contain ingredients that aren't harmful to dogs, as their digestive systems are different to ours.

A great way to diversify your product lines is to cater to dogs that have food intolerances. For example, some dogs are gluten-intolerant so create gluten-free options.

You can market your products at local flea markets, pet stores and retailers, veterinary

clinics, dog grooming salons, at pet fairs, or directly through an online storefront.

MONEY

SMALL BUSINESS OPPORTUNITIES ▪ MONEY MAKING IDEAS ▪ START YOUR OWN BUSINESS FOR BEGINNERS ▪ ESCAPE THE RAT RACE AND BE YOUR OWN BOSS

BUY A BUSINESS

Not everyone is keen on the idea of building a brand new business from the ground up. A new business means finding new customers to get the business rolling, sorting out business plans and operations models, and marketing your services to customers who may prefer to

MONEY
SMALL BUSINESS OPPORTUNITIES ■ MONEY MAKING
IDEAS ■ START YOUR OWN BUSINESS FOR BEGINNERS
■ ESCAPE THE RAT RACE AND BE YOUR OWN BOSS

buy from established brands rather than from a start-up.

By comparison, if you have the funding to do so, you can buy an existing business or purchase the franchising license for a well-established brand.

Turnkey Business

A turnkey business is one that is already established and operating. There are plenty of advantages of buying a turnkey business, but there are also a few disadvantages to consider.

Before you take the leap into buying a business that is already established, take a moment to consider the pros and cons.

Advantages

Most people automatically assume that buying an established business is less risky than starting a new business. You're able to view the financial history of the business and take over existing operations, so there should be

MONEY
**SMALL BUSINESS OPPORTUNITIES ■ MONEY MAKING
IDEAS ■ START YOUR OWN BUSINESS FOR BEGINNERS
■ ESCAPE THE RAT RACE AND BE YOUR OWN BOSS**

very little disruption in normal business. The primary advantages of buying a turnkey business are:

- ■Less risk associated with an established business than beginning a new start-up

- ■Business plans and procedures are already in place

- ■Immediate cash flow from continued operations

- ■Financial history already in place

- ■Existing customer base and contacts with suppliers, staff, equipment, and stock

- ■An established market for the product or services

- ■Existing employees can continue daily operations as required

Disadvantages

Not every business for sale on the market is a good investment. Many business owners may

MONEY

SMALL BUSINESS OPPORTUNITIES ■ MONEY MAKING
IDEAS ■ START YOUR OWN BUSINESS FOR BEGINNERS
■ ESCAPE THE RAT RACE AND BE YOUR OWN BOSS

be selling out of the business because the market may be unsteady. The industry may be on the decline, or the business may be under-performing. Many people believe that a struggling business being sold cheaply could represent a real bargain and an opportunity to build it back up to its real potential. However, there are some disadvantages to consider before buying a turnkey business, including:

■ Larger initial investment to get started as compared to starting a business from scratch

■ The existing business may need major financial contributions to update or replace old plan and equipment

■ The business may be operating in a poor location

■ The previous business owners may have developed a poor business reputation with past customers

MONEY

SMALL BUSINESS OPPORTUNITIES ■ MONEY MAKING
IDEAS ■ START YOUR OWN BUSINESS FOR BEGINNERS
■ ESCAPE THE RAT RACE AND BE YOUR OWN BOSS

■There may be bad managers or employees already within the business

■The business could be within a declining industry niche, which negatively affects future growth and expansion

Before investing into any business enterprise, it's vitally important to conduct your due diligence.

Franchise Business

Buying a franchise business means you have a well-known brand that operates under exactly the same business procedures as every other franchise outlet, so customers know what they're getting with your products or services.

However, there are always advantages and disadvantages to every business opportunity. Before you jump into a franchise business, consider some of the pros and cons. You should also note that not all franchise

opportunities will include or incorporate the factors listed below.

Advantages

Having access to an established way of doing business that replicates a certain customer experience is a definite bonus. After all, you can walk into any McDonalds store in Thailand or Australia and receive the same products and service as you'd get right here at home. Some of the biggest advantages to buying a franchise system include:

- Well-established brand, product, or service

- Full assistance from the franchisor with site selection, lease negotiation, site development, and shop fitters

- Assistance with finance options or securing finance from banks or other lenders

- Initial management training

- Ongoing management assistance

- Established standard business procedures, operating manuals, and stock control systems

- Established financial systems already in place

- Franchisor deals with marketing and advertising for the business

Disadvantages

Of course, while a franchise system sounds like an easy way to get started in business, there are always downsides to consider. Some of the biggest disadvantages include:

- Restricted territory in which you can operate or promote your business

- Ongoing payment of fees to the franchisor

- The franchisor is not obliged to renew your franchise agreement at the end of the franchise term

- Less autonomy in business decisions or addition of new product lines

MONEY

**SMALL BUSINESS OPPORTUNITIES ■ MONEY MAKING
IDEAS ■ START YOUR OWN BUSINESS FOR BEGINNERS
■ ESCAPE THE RAT RACE AND BE YOUR OWN BOSS**

■Selling your business may mean paying fees to the franchisor, reducing any profits you may have built up

■Restrictions on the sale or termination of the franchise

HOME CARE SERVICES

More people are realizing the benefits of providing care services from home. There are plenty of people out there who prefer the personalized touch. Home care services are also sometimes more affordable options than professional care services.

MONEY

SMALL BUSINESS OPPORTUNITIES ■ MONEY MAKING
IDEAS ■ START YOUR OWN BUSINESS FOR BEGINNERS
■ ESCAPE THE RAT RACE AND BE YOUR OWN BOSS

Here are some options you might consider:

Senior Care Services

Providing non-medical senior care services is a growing industry. After all, there are a lot of aging baby boomers out there that need non-medical assistance from day to day.

Some may require a responsible driver to provide transportation to attend appointments or to get the week's grocery shopping done. Some may want some assistance with meal preparation, handling, and cooking.

There are also seniors out there who will happily pay for concierge services, where you help run errands, deal with basic cleaning services, help with grooming and basic dressing needs, or help out with computer training or support.

Others may simply pay for a level of companion care, where you'll spend time with your clients completing puzzles, playing games, accompanying the person to fitness classes or taking a walk together to ensure the person's safety during exercise, or just providing important social interaction they otherwise wouldn't receive.

Of course, you can choose to run your business as the organizer and administrator while you oversee a staff of medically-trained professionals who provide more in-depth medication management, wound dressing and care, and other related types of care.

While many seniors will be lucid and active, there will be some that will suffer from infirmities and varying degrees of mental capacity.

Your job is to become a huge asset to your aging clients. You can do this by providing your own services. You can also help by providing information about various services that can make their lives easier.

MONEY

SMALL BUSINESS OPPORTUNITIES ■ MONEY MAKING
IDEAS ■ START YOUR OWN BUSINESS FOR BEGINNERS
■ ESCAPE THE RAT RACE AND BE YOUR OWN BOSS

Home-Based Daycare business

Home-based day care services are a great option for those people who have the time and energy to look after other people's kids. As a business owner, you can set your own hours based on your preferences.

The best part about running a home-based day care business is that you get to stay at home with your own kids while earning money. In most states, a home-based day care business can accept up to six children at one time, with no more than two children under the age of 2.

Starting your day care business doesn't require a large initial investment. However, if you're living in a rental property you may need to get permission from your landlord to operate a business from home.

MONEY

**SMALL BUSINESS OPPORTUNITIES ▪ MONEY MAKING
IDEAS ▪ START YOUR OWN BUSINESS FOR BEGINNERS
▪ ESCAPE THE RAT RACE AND BE YOUR OWN BOSS**

Space Requirements

You will need to check that your home has the minimum number of square feet of space per child in care according to your state's laws. Most states require a minimum of 35 square feet per child, as well as having a safe outdoor space for play areas. You can find out the requirements in your state by contacting the agency that deals with day care licensing in your area.

Activities and Care Options

Keep in mind that providing family day care services is much more than just babysitting other people's kids. You'll be required to provide play areas, fun activities to keep kids

SMALL BUSINESS OPPORTUNITIES ■ MONEY MAKING
IDEAS ■ START YOUR OWN BUSINESS FOR BEGINNERS
■ ESCAPE THE RAT RACE AND BE YOUR OWN BOSS

entertained, educational activities, quiet space for nap time, and meals.

If your service accepts very young children, you'll also be responsible for changing diapers and potty training.

Insurance

Your business will need to take out additional insurance to cover your home day care business. Some states may ask you to have CPR and first-aid certificates before you start accepting children. Other states may also require that you complete courses in child development, child abuse prevention, nutrition, and other health-related courses.

Business Policy and Contracts

Before you open for business, it's important to spend some time planning and organizing how you'll operate your business. Each child you accept into your home for day care services

MONEY

SMALL BUSINESS OPPORTUNITIES ■ MONEY MAKING
IDEAS ■ START YOUR OWN BUSINESS FOR BEGINNERS
■ ESCAPE THE RAT RACE AND BE YOUR OWN BOSS

will need to have a contract signed by the parents.

Your contract needs to include your business policies for payment, fees for any late payments or bounced checks, and charges for vacations, paid holidays and overtime.

Other things to include in your contract policies include sick children, scheduling and discipline rules. If you're not sure how to get started with your policies, contact your local home child-care licensing agency and ask for a sample contract.

MONEY

SMALL BUSINESS OPPORTUNITIES ■ MONEY MAKING IDEAS ■ START YOUR OWN BUSINESS FOR BEGINNERS ■ ESCAPE THE RAT RACE AND BE YOUR OWN BOSS

FLEA MARKET ENTREPRENEUR

Thinking about creating a retail business, but don't have the cash to get started? Why not consider your local flea market or swap meet as a cheap entry point into the market?

Flea markets provide the ideal environment to incubate a business idea. Art shows, craft fairs, flea markets, or farmers markets are excellent venues for growing and expanding a

MONEY

SMALL BUSINESS OPPORTUNITIES ■ MONEY MAKING IDEAS ■ START YOUR OWN BUSINESS FOR BEGINNERS ■ ESCAPE THE RAT RACE AND BE YOUR OWN BOSS

business idea or a hobby into a profitable retail business.

Most street fairs and markets have a very low entry cost. All you'll need is transport, a table, a cash box, your produces, and the fee to cover the cost of renting a small booth. Some states may also require you have a vendor's license, but the majority of flea markets provide vendors with plenty of information to help you get started.

Flea markets and swap meets are an excellent way to test the market for new business ideas. Vendors who set up at flea markets can gauge the market response for new products and check how various products fare with customer interest levels.

Many people who enjoy crafts and handmade goods do well at flea markets, as they're able to make their own products. However, they're sometimes limited to selling only as much as they can make.

Other vendors do very well buying products from wholesalers and selling them at retail prices directly to customers. The food and beverage side of the flea market business is also a highly profitable way to test new business ideas.

It's up to you whether you only want to operate on weekends on a part-time basis, or whether you aim at offering your products to a broader audience at daily swap meets.

Being at flea markets on a regular basis gives you the opportunity to be face-to-face with your customers. You have the opportunity to learn what they like about your business, what could be improved and what they would like to buy if you sold other items.

MONEY

SMALL BUSINESS OPPORTUNITIES ■ MONEY MAKING IDEAS ■ START YOUR OWN BUSINESS FOR BEGINNERS ■ ESCAPE THE RAT RACE AND BE YOUR OWN BOSS

Having a regular presence at a local flea market also means building up a loyal customer base. Most vendors have websites to showcase their products, along with online storefronts, and maintain a healthy online presence with customers following on various social media sites.

You also have a brilliant opportunity to learn from other vendors. More experienced vendors will often have tips and advice for newer people at the markets.

You can choose to stick to local flea markets as you build your business, or move around to other swap meets and markets in nearby areas to expand your customer base. You can also choose to offer your products for sale via an online storefront to help increase sales.

Perhaps the best part of operating a flea market business is having the opportunity to see whether your business idea will work for your goals. If standing behind a table at a flea market isn't your dream job, use your time to

build your customers, grow your product lines, and aim at opening a store when sales get big enough.

Million Dollar Business Case Study #3

It's surprising how many people underestimate the power of flea markets. Yet they remain a highly profitable way to start and test the strength of any retail business.

Back in 1998, Jack and Marilou Johar opened a small stall at the Paramount Swap Meet in California. They purchased good quality leather products from wholesalers and displayed them at various swap meets.

On their first day of business they sold $500 of product. Before long they expanded to a larger, permanent stall space at a daily swap meet in Anaheim, California.

By 2001, the couple were grossing around $10,000 per month in sales.

As the business grew, they tested new product lines in their swap meet stall and expanded their product line accordingly.

By 2005, the little flea market operation had grown into the Street Leathers Corp and moved into a wholesale warehouse space in Los Angeles that generates around $2.5 million in sales each year.

MONEY

SMALL BUSINESS OPPORTUNITIES ■ MONEY MAKING IDEAS ■ START YOUR OWN BUSINESS FOR BEGINNERS ■ ESCAPE THE RAT RACE AND BE YOUR OWN BOSS

CRAFTING AND HOMEMADE PRODUCTS

Do you have some skill at creating homemade crafted goods? There is a huge market out there for these types of items.

People love to buy homemade items, from blankets to sweaters to cute knitted toys, as they simply don't have the time to create these things themselves.

The benefit of creating a business around crafting ideas is that you can broaden your

MONEY

SMALL BUSINESS OPPORTUNITIES ■ MONEY MAKING
IDEAS ■ START YOUR OWN BUSINESS FOR BEGINNERS
■ ESCAPE THE RAT RACE AND BE YOUR OWN BOSS

clientele with multiple online outlets, as well as selling as local flea markets, farmer's markets, and craft fairs. People like to know that the items they're buying are hand-made by the designer or crafter, as it adds a touch of authenticity and uniqueness to the product.

There is a vast range of homemade products you can sell to make huge profits from home. Here are just some of them:

Knitting / Crocheting

If you enjoy knitting or crocheting, there are so many opportunities available for you to earn money. People love hand-made knitted or crocheted items and they're willing to pay a premium for you to make them.

Most people associate knitting with ugly Christmas sweaters and associate crochet with granny squares and lap blankets. However, modern patterns allow for knitting and crochet designs to create cute plushie toys, blankets, clothing, homeware items, accessories, and a

MONEY

SMALL BUSINESS OPPORTUNITIES ■ MONEY MAKING
IDEAS ■ START YOUR OWN BUSINESS FOR BEGINNERS
■ ESCAPE THE RAT RACE AND BE YOUR OWN BOSS

range of other items that are limited only by your imagination.

The problem with creating your business around only what you can make is that you're limited to the number of items you can create in a specified time frame.

Knitting and crocheting are both hobbies that take time and effort. If you're happy with the idea of earning a comfortable part-time income while you're watching TV in the evening, then it's a great option for you.

However, if you're keen to turn your hobby into a full-time enterprise, you may need to be a little more creative about ways to generate income.

For example, there are talented people out there who love to knit and crochet. They produce gorgeous items from their hobby that they sell for healthy profits. What those people may not realize is that they can also sell clearly-worded patterns for new designs to

MONEY

SMALL BUSINESS OPPORTUNITIES ■ MONEY MAKING
IDEAS ■ START YOUR OWN BUSINESS FOR BEGINNERS
■ ESCAPE THE RAT RACE AND BE YOUR OWN BOSS

other crafters so they can make the same items themselves.

Websites like Etsy.com, craftsy.com, and ravelry.com feature knitted and crocheted patterns that other crafters can purchase so they can do it themselves.

The small amount of money most designers charge to buy patterns seems unreasonable, especially considering the amount of work that goes into creating each pattern. However, if you consider multiple knitters and crocheters are always looking for new projects to work on, the sheer volume of sales could easily drive your income through the roof.

MONEY

SMALL BUSINESS OPPORTUNITIES ▪ MONEY MAKING IDEAS ▪ START YOUR OWN BUSINESS FOR BEGINNERS ▪ ESCAPE THE RAT RACE AND BE YOUR OWN BOSS

Sewing and Quilting Services

A home sewing business is a great way to earn some extra income from your sewing skills. If you're handy with simple clothing alterations or

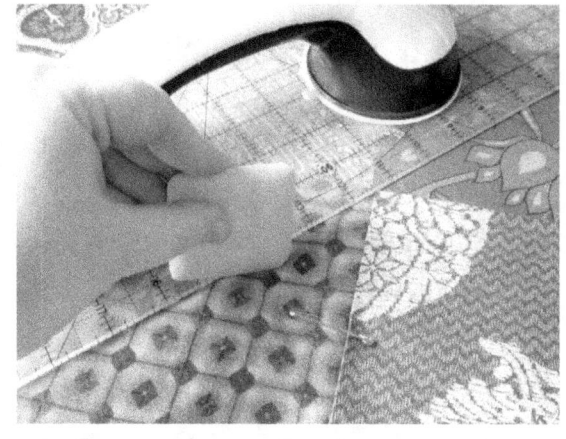

repairs, there are plenty of people out there who will want to take advantage of your services.

Of course, if you have a talent for dressmaking, you can advertise your services for creating made-to-order wedding dresses, bridal outfits, bridesmaid dresses, or even prom dresses. There's also the option of

MONEY

SMALL BUSINESS OPPORTUNITIES ■ MONEY MAKING IDEAS ■ START YOUR OWN BUSINESS FOR BEGINNERS ■ ESCAPE THE RAT RACE AND BE YOUR OWN BOSS

creating unique quilts, cushions, and other soft furnishings that are always in demand.

If you're creative, you can even make cute plush toys or matched kid's clothing sets. Build up some stock of your toys or clothing items and head down to the local craft fair to sell your products. You have the opportunity of advertising your primary dressmaking services at the same time as attracting new customers to your services.

You will need a robust sewing machine and an overlocking machine to get started. Promote your services on Etsy.com, using completed garments to show styles and then let customers know you'll take custom orders for people who want a garment in the same style.

MONEY
SMALL BUSINESS OPPORTUNITIES ■ MONEY MAKING
IDEAS ■ START YOUR OWN BUSINESS FOR BEGINNERS
■ ESCAPE THE RAT RACE AND BE YOUR OWN BOSS

Soap Making

Homemade soap-making businesses have the potential to grow into very profitable enterprises. People are becoming more concerned about the number of chemicals, artificial colors and fragrances, and synthetic ingredients in beauty products. There are also people out there with sensitive skin and allergies who often find it difficult to buy soap that won't irritate their skin.

Both of these things mean there's a huge market out there for good quality handmade soaps.

There are two primary methods for making soap. These are:

■ Cold process soap-making, which involves mixing an alkali with fats or oils, and then allowing the soap to cure for several weeks

MONEY

SMALL BUSINESS OPPORTUNITIES ■ MONEY MAKING IDEAS ■ START YOUR OWN BUSINESS FOR BEGINNERS ■ ESCAPE THE RAT RACE AND BE YOUR OWN BOSS

■Hot process soap-making, which involves cooking the soap

If you're willing to take the time to experiment with various soap recipes, organic ingredients, body-safe essential oils, and decorative soap molds, you could create a unique line of beautiful soaps that people will love.

Handmade soaps using organic ingredients sell very well at craft fairs, flea markets, farmer's markets, gift stores, and health food stores. You can expand your customer base by advertising your line of handmade soaps on a website or via social media.

MONEY

SMALL BUSINESS OPPORTUNITIES ■ MONEY MAKING
IDEAS ■ START YOUR OWN BUSINESS FOR BEGINNERS
■ ESCAPE THE RAT RACE AND BE YOUR OWN BOSS

Candle Making

Most people buy candles at some point in their lives, which has led to a boom in the popularity of specialty candles. They 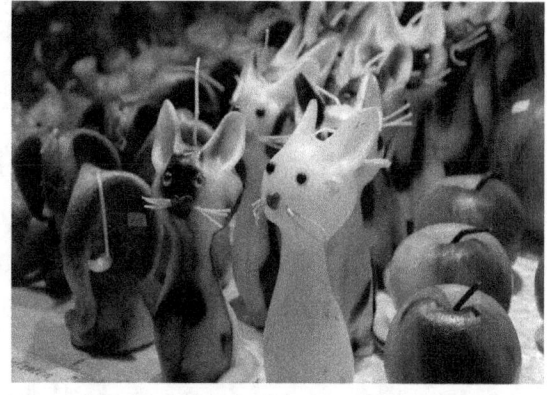 can be used for decorations, or to fill a room with a lovely scent as the candle burns, or for the relaxing aromatherapy effect they can give, or to create a romantic atmosphere over the dining table.

Making your own specialty homemade candles gives you the freedom to create unique designs and decorations with your products. You have the final say about which ingredients you use in your products, as well

as choosing the design for any packaging you use.

You'll need to have some candle making essentials on hand before you begin, including molds, melting pot, wax, wicks, essential oils and any other ingredients you want to use.

Homemade candles sell very well at craft fairs, flea markets, farmer's markets, and gift stores. Candles are also very popular items for church or college campus fundraisers and fairs, so if you can get organizers to purchase some of your products they'll sell quickly and come back to you again to buy more stock for their next fundraising event.

You can also promote your line of candles on your website or via social media networks to let people know what you're offering and how they can order from you.

MONEY

**SMALL BUSINESS OPPORTUNITIES ■ MONEY MAKING
IDEAS ■ START YOUR OWN BUSINESS FOR BEGINNERS
■ ESCAPE THE RAT RACE AND BE YOUR OWN BOSS**

Million Dollar Case Study #4

Sandie Ledray found that many commercial brands of soap irritated her sensitive skin, so she set about finding ways to make her own soap at home. She tested and experimented with a vast range of different soap making techniques and ingredients until she found combinations that worked for her.

Ledray focused on using all-natural products that contained no animal products or animal testing. Initially, her homemade soaps were made in her kitchen and sold to friends and family.

She expanded production and decided to market her soaps to other companies as a wholesaler. Her company, Brookside Soap Inc. now creates a line of private label soap for at least six other companies, who in turn market the soaps under their own brand names.

MONEY

SMALL BUSINESS OPPORTUNITIES ■ MONEY MAKING IDEAS ■ START YOUR OWN BUSINESS FOR BEGINNERS ■ ESCAPE THE RAT RACE AND BE YOUR OWN BOSS

Brookside Soap Inc. also sells its own brand-name products in health-food stores and gift shops and generates more than $200,000 a year in revenue.

MONEY

**SMALL BUSINESS OPPORTUNITIES ■ MONEY MAKING
IDEAS ■ START YOUR OWN BUSINESS FOR BEGINNERS
■ ESCAPE THE RAT RACE AND BE YOUR OWN BOSS**

BUSINESS SERVICES

For every business idea we've discussed in this book, there is a small business owner behind it trying to keep up with the bookkeeping tasks and financial management side of their business operations.

If you have the skills and qualifications, you could easily offer your services to them. With you taking care of the mundane paperwork side of the business or the online marketing

MONEY

SMALL BUSINESS OPPORTUNITIES ▪ MONEY MAKING IDEAS ▪ START YOUR OWN BUSINESS FOR BEGINNERS ▪ ESCAPE THE RAT RACE AND BE YOUR OWN BOSS

aspects, the small business owner suddenly has more free time to focus on working other facets of operations, which means generating more profits.

Bookkeeping

Being a good bookkeeper is all about understanding how a business works. If you're good at organizing financial information, your bookkeeping services could be in steady demand.

Your job will be to enter financial data into accounting software, keep track of accounts, including invoicing and receivables, tax preparation, payroll and bank reconciliation. Some business owners may also require assistance with risk management, strategic planning, and cash flow forecasting.

Contact small business owners in your local area and promote your services. Let them know you're willing to work on a contract basis, as they require the assistance, which

MONEY

SMALL BUSINESS OPPORTUNITIES ■ MONEY MAKING
IDEAS ■ START YOUR OWN BUSINESS FOR BEGINNERS
■ ESCAPE THE RAT RACE AND BE YOUR OWN BOSS

benefits their cash flow. Offer to tailor your services to suit their specific needs.

You may need to complete a bookkeeping course at a local community college. There are also certification programs available for Quickbooks or MYOB.

Accounting

Every business owner needs access to a good accountant, especially if they hope to stay in business for any length of time.

Your job is to take care of the business's bookkeeping, invoicing, accounts, payroll and bank reconciliations. Tax planning, preparation and filing are also in-demand services for a good accountant. You may also want to offer expert assistance with risk management, business planning, strategic planning, and financial advice.

MONEY

SMALL BUSINESS OPPORTUNITIES ■ MONEY MAKING IDEAS ■ START YOUR OWN BUSINESS FOR BEGINNERS ■ ESCAPE THE RAT RACE AND BE YOUR OWN BOSS

You will need to complete an accounting course and gain your certification before offering your services.

MONEY

**SMALL BUSINESS OPPORTUNITIES ▪ MONEY MAKING
IDEAS ▪ START YOUR OWN BUSINESS FOR BEGINNERS
▪ ESCAPE THE RAT RACE AND BE YOUR OWN BOSS**

CONCLUSION

No matter what type of business you choose to start, the key is to always treat your fledgling enterprise as a professional business at all times. Speak to a good accountant or business consultant about the best way to structure your business to help reduce taxes and ensure you have the right type of insurance to protect you at all times.

MONEY
SMALL BUSINESS OPPORTUNITIES ■ MONEY MAKING
IDEAS ■ START YOUR OWN BUSINESS FOR BEGINNERS
■ ESCAPE THE RAT RACE AND BE YOUR OWN BOSS

For some types of business, you'll need to complete a DBA, or 'doing business as' application through your local county administration office to register your business name. For others, you may need to set up an LLC or a company.

You'll also need to check any state or Local County permits and licensing requirements you need to conduct your business.

Take the time to work through an appropriate bookkeeping system for your business and stay on top of your entries regularly. After all, cash flow is your business's lifeblood, so it's important that your books are kept up to date to give you a clear idea of what your finances are doing at all times.

Work on building up your business's reputation with loyal customers and consider creating a website to establish a strong online presence.

Before you know it, you could be working in a thriving business as your own boss.

Other Available Books:

- In The Pursuit of Wisdom: The Principal Thing

- Investing in Gold and Silver Bullion - The Ultimate Safe Haven Investments

- Nigerian Stock Market Investment: 2 Books with Bonus Content

- The Dividend Millionaire: Investing for Income and Winning in the Stock Market

- Economic Crisis: Surviving Global Currency Collapse - Safeguard Your Financial Future with Silver and Gold

- Passionate about Stock Investing: The Quick Guide to Investing in the Stock Market

- Guide to Investing in the Nigerian Stock Market

- Building Wealth with Dividend Stocks in the Nigerian Stock Market (Dividends - Stocks Secret Weapon)

- Bitcoin and Digital Currency for Beginners: The Basic Little Guide

MONEY

SMALL BUSINESS OPPORTUNITIES ■ MONEY MAKING
IDEAS ■ START YOUR OWN BUSINESS FOR BEGINNERS
■ ESCAPE THE RAT RACE AND BE YOUR OWN BOSS

- Child Millionaire: Stock Market Investing for Beginners - How to Build Wealth the Smart Way for Your Child

- Christian Living: 2 Books with Bonus Content

- Beginners Quick Guide to Passive Income: Learn Proven Ways to Earn Extra Income in the Cyber World

- Taming the Tongue: The Power of Spoken Words

MONEY

SMALL BUSINESS OPPORTUNITIES ■ MONEY MAKING
IDEAS ■ START YOUR OWN BUSINESS FOR BEGINNERS
■ ESCAPE THE RAT RACE AND BE YOUR OWN BOSS

- The Power of Positive Affirmations: Each Day a New Beginning

- The Real Estate Millionaire: Beginners Quick Start Guide to Investing In Properties and Learn How to Achieve Financial Freedom

- Business: How to Quickly Make Real Money - Effective Methods to Make More Money: Easy and Proven Business Strategies for Beginners to Earn Even More Money in Your Spare Time

MONEY

SMALL BUSINESS OPPORTUNITIES ■ MONEY MAKING
IDEAS ■ START YOUR OWN BUSINESS FOR BEGINNERS
■ ESCAPE THE RAT RACE AND BE YOUR OWN BOSS

- Money: Think Outside the Cube: 2-Book
  Money Making Boxed Set Bundle
  Strategies

If you would like to share this book with
another person, please purchase an additional
copy for each recipient. Thank you for your
support and thanks for reading this book.

www.ingramcontent.com/pod-product-compliance
Lightning Source LLC
Chambersburg PA
CBHW060404190526
45169CB00002B/739